How
Self-I

C000163763

A 21-Day Blueprint to Develop Successful Habits,
Increase Your Productivity, Build Daily Self-Discipline
and Achieve Your Goals Faster

Judith Yandell

TABLE OF CONTENTS

What Is Self-Discipline?

Congratulations on purchasing *How to Build Self-Discipline* and thank you for doing so.

The following chapters will outline a 21-day plan that will transform your life and help you achieve new heights of productivity and happiness. Self-discipline is at the core of any successful life. In order to be able to do the things that you want to do, you will need self-discipline.

This first chapter will discuss what self-discipline is and why it is so helpful.

Self-discipline is simple, at its core. Self-discipline is the ability to do what you tell yourself to do. It is the assurance that if you make a plan to do something, you will do it. It seems so straightforward when framed like that. A dog will sit when you tell him to. But, for human beings, it is quite difficult.

Most people do not have the consistent ability to do what they tell themselves to do. Think of how common it is for someone to start a diet in January, as a New Year's Resolution, and then fail to keep to it by March. I'm sure you have met many people who dream big and have enormous plans for what they are going to do but never end up doing it.

The only thing holding people back is themselves. We often tell ourselves that bad luck in our life is due to our circumstances or situation, but that isn't true. Anyone can succeed and anyone is capable of changing their life. The critical feature is self-discipline.

Research shows that self-discipline is one of the most important features for success. A study by Angela Duckworth at the University of Pennsylvania found that self-discipline was more than twice as important as IQ for predicting academic performance for eighth graders. A giant study followed 1,000 children from birth to the age of thirty-two and found that childhood self-discipline predicted adult health, substance addiction, personal finances, and crime.

Self-discipline can help you in any part of your life, from your grades to your physical health.

A lot of people feel like they are constantly battling themselves. You might want to do the right thing, but you make the wrong choices anyway. Instead of the fruit that you know you should eat, you have a Twinkie. The ancient philosopher Aristotle called this the "weakness of the will." This is when we know what we should do, but can't make ourselves do it.

Self-discipline is about winning the conflict between the things that you want to do in the short term and the things that you know you should do in the long term. "Should" behaviors are things that will help your life in meaningful ways, like sleeping enough, eating well, doing your work, getting enough exercise, and studying. The behaviors that you want to do are more fun in the short term: junk food, video games, and sitting on the couch watching TV. When you pick the long-term goal instead of the attractive short-term distraction, you have exerted self-discipline.

Self-discipline, in a sense, is about the conflict between multiple different types of "self." You have the self in the present that wants the cookie and you have your future self, which will benefit if you do not eat that delicious cookie. This is why it is so common to make the choice to gratify your desires while telling yourself that you will never do that again. You are fulfilling the goals of your present self while projecting the ability to control yourself into the future. Future-you will have the ability to resist the cookie, even though present-you cannot.

Another way to think of it is that we are all always composed of selves with different priorities. There is the part of you that is present-oriented and focused on what you can do right now, versus the part of you that is the "planner" and future-oriented. Self-discipline is about the conflict between those two selves—are you staying focused on the present or are you able to create plans toward the future?

What is at the core of increasing self-discipline? This book will talk about a variety of specific strategies, but science tells us that self-discipline increases in two basic ways: either you can modify the *situation* or you can modify the way you *think* about the situation you are in. By modifying the situation, you remove barriers which make it harder to pick the right choice. For instance, if you always find yourself eating junk food instead of vegetables, a good step to improve self-discipline would be to not buy junk food anymore and not have it in the house. Modifying your thinking makes it more likely that you pick the right choice, even when you have the same options in front of you.

Habits are those things that you do automatically. We all have a huge number of habits in your life. Think about your commute—you don't have to consciously make all those choices about what turn to take, you just automatically do it. Habits are composed of **cues** and **rewards**. Cues are the triggers that initiate the behavior. We are cued by *time* and *place*. Our brain is triggered by a particular circumstance to engage in the behavior.

After the behavior happens, successful habits have *rewards*. This is how the behavior becomes reinforced and automatic. A great example is brushing your teeth. Historically, brushing teeth did not catch on until toothpaste was flavored in a pleasant minty way. The reward of your mouth tasting minty and fresh is what reinforces the behavior of brushing your teeth.

In order to create good habits, you have to control both the cues and rewards. You need to keep the cues easy at hand and you need to reward yourself for doing the thing that you want to do. If you want to walk more, leave your sneakers out so that you see them and are easily cued by them. And, instead of walking by a busy road, walk in a park so you have the pleasant sights and sounds as a reward.

These tricks will help you establish the habits that this book will talk about.

The 21-Day Project

The core of this book is a 21-day project of self-improvement. The way this works is that you will have something to focus on each day and each day will develop some of the skills necessary to make your life more productive and happy. Three weeks is not a long time, but it is plenty of time to help you start the process of reshaping your life. This 21-day project will help you achieve your goals and push yourself into being the best person you can be.

A critical part of success will be to be self-aware and self-critical throughout this entire process. An important way to do that is to establish the habit of *journaling*.

Keystone habits are habits that once established, can have a ripple effect throughout your entire life. They are habits that are small changes with big effects. A true keystone habit has the ability to spark a series of positive changes throughout your entire life.

The best and most important keystone habit is *journaling*. Keeping a personal journal is the best way to keep aware of your mental state and keep accountable to your inner life. Journaling has been used by great people from Benjamin Franklin to Albert Einstein. Countless people have used a daily journal to help structure their lives since time immemorial.

Journaling is the regular reflection on your life by writing things down, whether that be on a physical notebook or a file on your computer. I would urge you, at least to start, in using an actual book. The tangible qualities of pen and paper help your mind really process what you are writing in a way that typing cannot match.

Learning to spend time reflecting on your life is at the core of self-discipline. As we discussed in the last chapter, the whole problem of self-discipline is about how to motivate yourself to take your long-term goals more seriously than surface level distractions in the present. The way to do that is to keep the long-term goals close to mind and easily accessible.

Further, without a regular habit of journaling, it is much harder to keep track of what you are actually doing. Journaling forces you to look at your life in an objective way, analyzing what you've actually done and what you want to do. It keeps you accountable.

So, for this three-week project (and hopefully beyond) start a journal. Purchase a book that feels nice to you and is attractive. Like all habits, you should make journaling pleasant and rewarding. Use a nice journal and a nice pen, something that feels good to use. Get in the habit of taking some time out, every day, to reflect on what you have done that day and what you want to do.

Many of the activities proposed in the following pages will involve journaling and writing. The most powerful organ we have is our brain and in order to do anything valuable, we need to get our brain on our side. Our thoughts control, in a meaningful way, what we actually do. We cannot make changes without first changing our mind. This means that the tool of journaling is crucial, because it is an excellent way of knowing and changing our own minds.

The first thing you are going to do is you should motivate why you are going to engage in this 21-day project. It would be much easier to just continue your normal life and your normal routine, whatever it is. Inertia is a powerful thing and the habits you currently have were certainly established because they were attractive in some way. You get something out of the way you currently live. In order to change that, you have to keep in the forefront of your mind what you will get out of changing that life.

Take some time to think about your life. Write about what your current patterns are and what you currently do. If you have time, maybe take a few days before you start the 21-day plan to record what your normal habits and day-to-day routine is. What does your life look like now?

Once you have a clear picture of your current life, then think about what is deficient about it? Why did you buy this book? What do you want to change? Think about the ways in which your current patterns hold you back and make things more difficult for you. If you can, think of specific opportunities that your current habits made you miss or squander. Really get into the impacts of your lack of self-discipline and the things that make it harder for you to achieve your goals.

Then, after you've done all that, imagine what you could do if you had self-discipline. What are your dreams? What do you want to change? Take some time imagining them, in as great detail as you can. Spend the time really visualizing what it would be like to be more productive, more capable, and more self-sufficient.

Self-discipline, by nature, is about sacrifice. It is about giving up the pleasures of today for greater happiness in the future. In order to motivate that, you need a clear and strong picture of what you are working for. Use this time preparing for your 21-day plan to create that picture for yourself.

Writing this all down keeps it more concrete and real for you. It will force you to actually spend time with it and keep it close at hand. Without actually writing it down, your goals will be ephemeral and hard to keep track of.

Before you begin the three weeks, make sure to read over the whole book and make note of anything you will need to plan in advance. I have tried to make sure that all of the tasks can at least be begun in the day they are listed, but it is often useful to know what it is coming.
Finally, make sure you've made a commitment to yourself to keep going. This will be difficult. Sometimes you will struggle. But you have to promise yourself that you are going to work hard and keep pushing on to your goals. Keep that image of your new, self-productive life close at hand. You can do this. The point is to push yourself and stretch your self-discipline. This will make you stronger.

The Daily Routine

We will be dealing with a lot of complicated ideas and concepts which will be helpful for your personal development and growth. At the base, though, some of the most important things you can do are to establish a routine that prioritizes the basic elements of self-care. If the fundamentals of your life aren't in order, it will be much harder to achieve higher goals. You cannot excel in work or in school if you aren't taking care of your body— or, if you think you can, you will find that you are limited by that lack of self-care.

This chapter will talk about the basic daily routine that will help you succeed in anything you want to do.

Perhaps the most important element is getting enough *sleep*. Sleep has enormous effects on every part of our lives, but it especially has effects on our ability to think. When you aren't getting enough sleep, your brain doesn't work as well. Lack of sleep means that you will be slower to respond and have less alertness. You will not have the ability to pay close attention to tasks that require it. Any higher order cognitive task will be hurt by lack of sleep, including anything that requires creativity and innovation. Even emotional capacity is decreased by not sleeping enough.

One of the most important things you can do to ensure that you have enough good sleep is to stick to a daily routine about when you go to sleep and when you wake up. You should pick a bedtime and a time to wake up that gives you a good eight hours of sleep. Once you have picked it, stick to it. I would suggest waking up early enough that you have several hours before you have to leave for work in the morning. Those morning hours are a crucial time for you to get stuff done.

In addition, make sure that you increase bright light exposure during the day and decrease it at night. Our ability to sleep is in part determined by our body's internal biological clock. This clock is regulated by hormones, which are regulated by our exposure to light. Our internal clock determines day time by how much light we receive and night time by a decrease of light. This means that you have to make sure to spend some time outside each day in order to make sure you get a maximum amount of sun. At night, try to avoid using your many devices close to bedtime. All electronics produce a bright blue light, which replicates the light of the sun to our minds and bodies. When you are on your phone at night, you are confusing your body and making it more difficult to sleep. As part of your routine, pick a time a few hours before your bedtime at which point you will no longer use electronics.

Just before bed, establish a relaxation routine that prepares you for sleep. Techniques like deep breathing or meditation (discussed in depth on Day 6) can help you settle down and help you sleep. Other relaxing activities like listening to music or reading a book can help you calm down. Make sure to create space for calm and quiet before bedtime.

In addition to sleep, exercise and movement are crucial to a well-balanced and nourished life. Exercise does not only help you sleep, but it also helps you in all aspects of your health and well-being. Getting enough exercise will help you think better and it will help you live longer. It will also make you feel better, as research shows that physical activity is linked to better mood.

In general, pushing yourself to do physical activities helps you stretch your self-discipline. Physical exercise is difficult and pushing yourself to do it will increase your ability to do difficult things.

Find time in your day to do at least thirty minutes of exercise each and every day. This exercise does not have to be super intense, but you should increase your heart rate and make sure your blood is pumping. Take a walk or jog with your dog; lift some weights. If you would like, find a class that you can take to really push yourself. This will not only increase your physical and mental health, but it will also help you achieve all sorts of other goals.

In addition, always take the stairs and find as many opportunities as you can to walk. Instead of driving, walk. If you have to drive, park far away, so you have to walk the last bit. Take regular breaks where you walk around and get some movement. Most of us spend far too much time still and we don't stretch our bodies.

Another important element of our physical health is how we eat. You are literally made of what you put into your body. The protein and fat that you consume is the fuel that lets you think and move. When you eat unhealthily, you are contributing to negative health outcomes like obesity. Make sure to eat plenty of fruit and even more vegetables. Most of your diet should be vegetables, as they have many nutrients and are very good for you. While you shouldn't cut out fat entirely, try to avoid excessive fat. Choose lean proteins and low-fat dairy. In general, most people should eat less meat. Meat is associated with harmful health outcomes such as colon cancer.

The last part of your daily routine is something that we have already discussed: journaling. Reserve time each morning to journal about what you want to do that day. Set forward goals and outcomes that you want to achieve in the coming day. At night, write down what you did that day and reflect on what was successful about the choices you made. Take this time to analyze yourself and understand what it is that you are doing with your time.

After reading this chapter, write out in your journal your daily routine. Write down when you will wake up, when you will exercise, when you will journal, when you will eat, and when you will go to sleep. Set timers on your phone, if that will help you. Make a commitment to stick to this daily routine. Most truly disciplined people have a strong daily routine that has all the elements discussed in this chapter. Make it a goal that you establish one.

Day 1:
Setting Good Goals

We all have things that we want to do in life. A key task of self-discipline is learning to articulate these goals in a sensible way that will help us actually achieve them. Just vaguely wanting things does not help you achieve the things that you want to do.

Goals should be SMART: specific, measurable, attainable, relevant, and time-bound. These are features that all good goals should have. When you create goals, make sure they meet these five features. We will go through these qualities one by one.

Good goals should be **specific**. You should be able to answer a lot of specific questions about the goal. What do you want to achieve? Who is involved in this goal? Where is this goal? Which resources will you need to achieve this goal? Instead of being vague when you discuss your goals, always define exactly what you want. A good goal is never what you want to be "successful"—always define what success means to you and what it looks like. Instead of wanting success in your career, declare that you want to be promoted to management.

The outcomes that you want should be **measurable**. You should be able to exactly determine and track what you want to achieve. This will help you stay focused because you will know your progress and you will be able to exactly tell if you have met your goal. It is much harder to be motivated to work toward a goal if you do not know if you have met it. Instead of the goal to "write more," you should have the goal to write a certain amount of words or pages.

When you pick a measurable outcome, make sure that it is **achievable**. Setting goals that are too high can be discouraging and it changes how we think about goals. Goals should be something that you plan to actually *do*. If you set pie-in-the-sky goals, then you will not be motivated to actually get things done. They should always be within the realm of possibility, even if they are difficult.

One thing that makes goals achievable is that they are *process-based* as opposed to *outcome-based*. The thing about outcomes is that many aspects of them are outside of your control. You cannot always guarantee that the world will be in the configuration that you want it to be or that other people will act in the way that you want them to. Even a goal like "getting a job" depends on things that other people do. Process-based goals are about what you do and therefore, are always achievable. If you set the goal of submitting a job application each day, you know you will be able to achieve that. It does not depend on anything but yourself. This means it is within your power.

Your goal should also be **relevant**. This means that it is important to you and fits in the view of what you want in your life. If you set goals that aren't sincere or that feel artificial, it will be much harder for you to meet them. Relevant goals are worthwhile. It is the right time for them and they are compatible with your other goals. For instance, if you have the goal of a particular job, but that job would require a move, you might decide that you do not actually want that because it does not feel worth it to you to uproot your family.

Goals should be **time-bound**, which means that they need a target date and a deadline. Without a deadline, it is much harder to work to achieve your goals. They become vague and serve to just increase a general sense of stress as opposed to feeling like something that you will actually complete.

Once you have constructed these goals, determine a way that you can **record** them and keep track of your progress. If you have a goal of finishing a project, have a part in your journal where you keep track of your project and give yourself milestones. If you want to lose weight, regularly weigh yourself and determine what your progress has been.

This is the general theory about creating good goals. Once you understand that, the next step is to refine your actual goals into meeting these criteria. Take some time today to sit down and come up with your goals. The first step should be to brainstorm what you want your life to look like. What would be different in your perfect life? What would be different about yourself, your home, your job? What do you want to achieve? Take some time to really think about this and to dwell on what makes life valuable for you.

Once you have that general list of brainstormed goals, pick three things to work on. It is impossible to change everything at once, so make sure to focus on what is most important and accessible. As a rule of thumb, these three things should include at least one goal that is short-term and more easily achievable.

At that point, refine these three goals into being SMART. They should be specific, measurable, achievable, relevant, and time-bound. If in the process of doing this, you determine that the goals aren't actually achievable or relevant, go back to the drawing board and replace them with something that feels more authentic and possible.

Write these three goals in a place of pride in your journal. For some people, they might find it valuable to write them up on a piece of paper and post them on the wall or the fridge. Keep these goals in mind and make sure that you are organizing your life so that you can achieve them.

After you have determined the goals, pick one of them that seems the most achievable and break it down into steps. What are the intermediate parts that you will need to do in order to achieve this goal? What should the timeline be for each of those steps? Make a timeline for yourself and enter it into your calendar. Determine what changes to your life you will need to make to be able to achieve your goal.
And then, once you have done all that, make a commitment to actually getting it done.

Day 2:
Anticipating and Solving Problems

Everybody encounters problems and problem-solving skills can be learned! There are ways of thinking about problems which make you better at solving them. The most important thing is to establish a "positive problem orientation." This means that you view problems as a challenge that is possible to improve. You believe that you have the ability to solve problems and you acknowledge that successful problem solving will have instances of failure. Not every problem will be solved with the first attempt, but that doesn't mean that problems cannot be solved.

A negative problem orientation, on the other hand, views problems as unsolvable and frightening. If you have this orientation, you view problems as impossible to improve and you do not think that you have the ability to solve problems. Any failure means that failure is inevitable.

A positive problem orientation means that you view difficulties as normal life challenges and you try to find solutions. This optimism can be learned and is, essentially, a choice. Act optimistic and look for new possibilities. When you strive to look for solutions to your problems, you will find that this optimism becomes more and more natural.

Your first task is to start the process of creating a positive problem orientation. Whenever you think of something negative, force yourself to rephrase the thought and find possibilities. Never let yourself be pessimistic without a correction. Make a commitment to solving problems.

Problem-solving has four steps:
1) Identify the problem and set goals.
2) Determine possible solutions.
3) Evaluate the solutions and decide which one you are going to try.
4) Try the solution and after you try it, determine how well it worked and if it did solve the problem.

One way to practice that is to actually try to solve problems! Think of a problem in your life. Problems are things that cause you pain and difficulty. This can be a problem in your personal life, your work, your school, or your health. In the process of identifying the problem, it is a good idea to be as specific as possible. Being clear makes it much easier to think of solutions.

Ask yourself questions like what happened to bother you? Who is involved in the problem? Why is this problem difficult for you? Really isolate the problem situation and what the goals should be. Remember, when you set a goal, the goal should be SMART: specific, measurable, achievable, relevant, time-bound.

Once you have a clear sense of the problem and the goal that you have in fixing it, the next step is to brainstorm solutions. It is often difficult to approach solving a problem, which makes sense because if it was easy, you might have already fixed it! Problem-solving means pushing yourself outside your comfort zone and thinking in new ways. In order to do that, you have to generate as many solutions as possible. Don't worry about if they are feasible or impossible. Defer judgment entirely on if they are good solutions. First, you simply have to think of them. Write down a list of possible solutions to your problems.

Ask yourself what you would tell someone else if they had this problem. Or, alternately, what would someone you love tell you to do to solve this problem? Are there strategies you use in other parts of your life that could help with this problem?

Once you have the list of solutions, you then need to examine them and determine their pros and cons. Evaluate the likelihood that the solution will succeed in solving the problem and meeting your goals. Also, make sure to keep in mind any other effects the solution may have. What are the short and long term benefits and drawbacks of each problem? Consider how the solution will affect not only you but other people as well.

Then, select a solution and make a plan. Solutions need to be implemented in order to solve anything. Plans should be as specific as you can make them in order to make it possible to do them. Write out what you will do, day by day, being specific as to the time and place.

One way to prepare for solving a problem is to "rehearse it" in your mind. Use your imagination to visualize actually carrying out the solution. What do you need to do? What will it feel like? Use this process to imagine possible difficulties and what you would do to solve them.

Try out your solution! This will be an experiment, like a scientist, where you try something and see what happens. Even if it doesn't work, you will learn something from the attempt. Failure does not mean failure forever, all it means is that you have to go back to your list of brainstormed solutions and try another one, now knowing more about the situation.

Another exercise you can do to anticipate problems is called a "pre-mortem." Most of us do "post-mortems," where we look at something that has already failed and try to fix it. A useful exercise is to try to do this in advanced. Try it out for this three-week project. Imagine that you have failed in your goal of following the three-week plan for self-discipline. Why have you failed? What are the most likely scenarios for a failure? What might get in the way of success?

Make a list of possibilities that could get in your way and brainstorm how you can prevent them, using the four steps that we discussed before. Use problem-solving, not just to solve problems that have already happened but to prevent problems in the future. This will help you achieve your many goals, not just in the fulfillment of this three-week program, but also in the rest of your life.

As a reminder, when you are going through these mental exercises, take the time to write them down. The brain learns better when it has to dwell on its thoughts and feelings. You will be well-served by writing down what you want to learn. This is especially true in the case of problem-solving, because if the proposed solution does not work, you want to be able to go back to your brainstormed list of possibilities to try another one.

Day 3:
Reward Yourself for Success

Self-discipline isn't about punishing yourself. It is about making yourself better. Human beings learn best through *positive reinforcement* instead of negative reinforcement. The concept of "reinforcement" comes from experiments conducted by a scientist named BF Skinner. He was a psychologist studying human behavior. His research showed that behavior which is reinforced tends to continue. Behavior which is punishing or has negative outcomes tends to fall away. This means that, if we want to encourage good behavior, we need to have the ability to reinforce it.

When you reinforce a behavior, you increase the likelihood that you do that behavior. Negative reinforcement works as well, but it works out of fear. When you study in order to avoid getting an "F," that is negative reinforcement. If you clean your room so that your mom doesn't yell at you, that is also negative reinforcement. Negative reinforcement is inevitable, but establishing patterns of positive reinforcement will make your life more pleasant and agreeable.

One thing to be careful of is to not let positive reinforcement and rewards destroy your *intrinsic motivation*. Intrinsic motivation is the reasons you do something for its own sake. They are the rewards that come naturally from doing the behavior. Intrinsically enjoyable activities like eating, playing games, and spending time with those you love don't have to be rewarded because they come with their own reward. It is pleasant to do them, so you want to do them. Many things are naturally intrinsically rewarding. Some of those things you do to excess because they are so pleasurable—eating and playing games can be examples of that.

Some things we do, however, are less obviously intrinsically motivating. Self-discipline, as discussed, is about doing difficult things instead of the easy, obvious thing that is right in front of us. Our work, for example, is often difficult. It can be hard to find intrinsic motivation for doing difficult things.

However, your first task is to look for things you find satisfying about even difficult things. Make a list of things in your life that are difficult or unpleasant. This list will differ depending on your preferences and is different for each person. Exercise, cleaning, writing emails—all of these things might be on the list.

When you have the list of things that you find difficult, take some time to think about ways they are *intrinsically rewarding*. What are elements of these tasks that you find enjoyable? To take the example of cleaning, there might be something pleasant about seeing something dirty become clean. Or, more mundanely, you might like the smell of your favorite cleaning product. When doing laundry, you might like the warmth of things right out of the dryer. Try to brainstorm elements of all the difficult tasks you do that you can focus on and try to enhance as more beneficial.

Once you have things you find intrinsically rewarding, try to find ways to accentuate these positive elements. Find even nicer smelling cleaning supplies, for instance. Or if when writing emails, you find the empty mailbox satisfying, find a mail program that encourages you to get to "inbox zero." If you like the satisfying feeling of words ticking up when you are writing, use a program that prominently displays the word count of your text. For each of your difficult tasks, think of one or two ways you can accentuate their intrinsic rewards.

You will probably find that even with intrinsic rewards, some tasks are still more difficult than others. This is inevitable. Life isn't always easy and it isn't supposed to be. In order to push yourself to do these hard things, it is useful to come up with ways to positively reinforce these behaviors and come up with easy, guilt-free rewards for doing them.

One important strategy for doing difficult tasks is to create behavioral contracts where you link specific rewards to specific good behavior. If you do a hard thing, you can automatically do a thing that you like in response. For instance, if going to medical appointments is hard and stressful for you, maybe you reward yourself for going by going to the bookstore and getting something new each time. Or, perhaps, you can watch your favorite show when you are on the treadmill. The usefulness of these things is that they can become automatic. Go to the list of difficult tasks that you came up with earlier in this chapter and come up with behavioral contracts for several of them. What things can you link together to make the more difficult thing easier to do? If you are trying to lose weight and you collect something, maybe you can only buy that item when you lose five pounds. Or, perhaps, if you struggle to do laundry, maybe you can listen to an audiobook that you enjoy while you fold. Encourage yourself to do good behavior by linking something pleasant with that behavior.

In addition, you should create a list of guilt-free rewards that you can use whenever you have to do something difficult. Everybody has hard days or hard tasks that you just need to do, even though you really don't want to. It is useful to have a list of things that you can promise yourself to encourage the difficult thing that you are trying to avoid. Possibilities include going to the movies, dinner at a favorite restaurant, a small piece of candy, buying something that you want, reading a fun novel, buying a magazine, listening to a favorite album, calling a good friend.... Anything that you enjoy can become a reward. The goal is to create a list of things that you can do at any time, with minimal constraints, so you can always deploy them as incentives.

With more long-term tasks and goals, think of progressive rewards that you can use at individual milestones. Even though it feels childish, something like a reward chart where you give yourself a sticker every day you do a new habit can be very effective. Even small rewards can be useful if done regularly.

Day 4:
Find Meaning in Your Life

We have talked a lot about concrete goals and problems in your life. Everything we have said so far has been about being as specific and realistic as possible. In that line, looking for meaning might seem wishy-washy and irrelevant. However, research shows that having a strong sense of meaning in your life is crucial to being self-disciplined and effective.

Self-discipline is about prioritizing long-term goals over short term pleasures. The ability to prioritize those goals depends on having a commitment to their importance and value. The way this works is to instill a strong sense of meaning in your life. You have to know why you are doing something and for what purpose.

Meaning is about fitting together the events and ideas in your life into a coherent whole. It is about telling a narrative of yourself as a person that you can understand and support, in the same way that a novel or a movie tells a story that makes sense to you.

Basically, all sources of meaning are determined in part by the people around you. Your individual relationships with your family and friends can be a crucial source of meaning. In a broader sense, our social and cultural life helps communicate to us what is important in life and how we should conceptualize ourselves. Some people find meaning in being parents or spouses. Others, in their bowling league or church group. Either way, one of the most crucial ways to find meaning is to reach out and make a human connection.

We have a need for **purpose**. We have talked in previous chapters about the importance of specific, concrete goals. Those goals need to be placed in an overall sense of your life as a project. Why do you choose the goals that you choose? For some people, their purpose is about achieving ambitions in their career. Another person might find purpose in being a father. The specific goals that those two people will try to achieve might look very different.

Having a sense of meaning gives a reason to do things and helps us feel fulfilled once we have done them. When we have meaning and purpose, the things that we do feel important. It becomes easier to force ourselves to do difficult things when it feels like those difficult things are in favor of a global life goal.

How do you find your purpose? One of the best ways is to develop your connection to others and the world around you. Reach out and explore the relationships you have with people around you. In addition to real, live people, try making a human connection through *reading*. Reading allows you to "interact" with people across time and space, in very different lives than your own. It can help you gain perspective on what you want in your own life.

When you read about somebody's whole life, that helps you gain perspective on your own without having to live it out yourself. A novel introduces you to the whole arc of life. With that in front of you, the sense of life that you want to lead can become more clear.

In addition, it is also useful to turn things that cause you pain in your life into a part of your sense of purpose. If you struggled as a child, that suffering can be something which drives you to help others. Many people who escaped poverty or ill-health find themselves drawn to preventing those harms from hurting others. This is a way to make difficult memories feel valuable or useful. If something that hurt you can end up being the impetus to help others, the pain might feel less.

Another strategy is to cultivate positive emotions like awe, gratitude, and generosity. It might seem counter-intuitive to look for the purpose by increasing your gratitude, but research has shown the experience of gratitude is associated with having a sense of yourself in the world. The ability to count your blessings and recognize all the gifts you have been given makes you more likely to help others and make an impact on the world. One of the best ways to acquire a sense of purpose is helping others. It is certainly possible to get purpose from self-interested pursuits, but it can be less fulfilling and sometimes feel empty. What is the point in getting a raise, on its own terms? If that raise will help you give your children a better life, on the other hand, it can feel much more important.

In a similar way, focusing on what other people find valuable about you and what you have done can help you find purpose. Pay attention to what other people appreciate about you and the work that you are already doing. Many people have had the experience of being surprised by praise or appreciation. Use that praise as a guide to continue doing what you are doing and push yourself to be someone that contributes in many ways to the world.

This is all part of the process of finding and building a community. Other people are where most of us find meaning. This can be explicitly altruistic, like non-profit work or teaching. It can also be more about the types of experiences and connections that any community makes. Even your video game clan can be a source of meaning if you cultivate it as a community. If you have trouble having a sense of purpose, look at the people around you. What do you have in common with those in your life? What are those people trying to do? Is there an impact on the world that you see them making? How can you be part of it? Take advantage of strong and purposeful people who are already in your life.

Finally, an excellent way to find purpose is to create. Writing especially is a good way to find meaning in the things that you do. We need to be able to make a narrative about our lives and give ourselves a sense of going somewhere for some reason. Writing down what we value and what is important to us can be a crucial part of that process. Individuals who have a greater purpose in their life tend to be able to tell a story about themselves that explains how their troubles have to lead to greater meaning. There is a story of change and overcoming that you can tell about your life— find it.

Daily journaling can be a crucial part of this process. Taking the time to analyze what you are doing and why you are doing it helps to increase the sense of yourself as someone with meaning and purpose.

Today, you should spend some time thinking about the possible sources of meaning and purpose in your life. Write about it, considering the people and communities that are important to you. What activities feel *right* and like you are doing what you are meant to be doing?

Once you have a sense of that, write down your life story as if it was a story someone was telling. Explain how the disparate parts of your life fit together. It is important to make this a happy story and a tale of overcoming. You have undergone obstacles to get here, even if you aren't exactly where you want to be. How have you triumphed? Can you tell your story as one of success? Today, make an effort to write it down.

Day 5:
Tolerate Discomfort

Much of modern life is about searching for comfort in as many ways as possible. We have plush, soft beds. We are rarely too warm or too cold. Most of us have not experienced true, unpleasant hunger. Resources are in abundance and surround us all the time.

If you are someone who has experienced real discomfort, you know that it can be difficult to deal with. Discomfort is uncomfortable! This seems obvious, but it is at the core of why we so often take the easy road instead of the hard one. Because many difficult things are uncomfortable, even though we want to achieve the goals that require them, we shy away from that discomfort.

In many ways, self-discipline is about learning to tolerate discomfort. When we exert self-discipline, we make an effort to choose the difficult thing instead of the easy one. We work out in the early morning, even though it would be more comfortable to sleep. We make our muscles sore and tire out our body. We eat the spartan, plain food instead of delicious stuff like pasta and meatballs.

The ability to tolerate discomfort is associated with success in meeting difficult goals. Smokers who had better abilities to tolerate discomfort were more likely to be able to quit smoking, which is a profound test in self-discipline.

The ability to tolerate discomfort is something that can be improved. It is like a muscle—pushing yourself and learning to stretch your ability to tolerate discomfort makes it easier to tolerate the discomfort in the future. When you know you have survived something in the past, it becomes much more approachable to survive it again. When we focus too much on our desire to be comfortable and treat discomfort as a catastrophe, it becomes much harder to deal with whatever is happening.

The attitude you need to cultivate is that discomfort is not that big of a deal. Discomfort is a normal part of life. It is not a problem or a failure to have uncomfortable things happen to you. Think of your primitive ancestors, who hunted and gathered for their food. For them, hunger was not a failure. It was a normal part of the process. Sometimes you would be fully fed and sometimes you would be hungry. The experience of hunger did not mean anything went wrong.

Because of the comforts of modern life, many of us things that any experience of physical unpleasantness means that something has gone wrong. Discomfort is to be corrected. But discomfort only becomes a problem when you convince yourself that it is a problem. Do not allow the thought that life must be comfortable to take root. When you struggle with the fact that you are experiencing pain, you will also have painful emotions which makes everything worse.

Of course, discomfort is unpleasant. That is basically the definition. But you can deal with it. A little hunger, or soreness, or cold—none of those things will kill you. Most forms of discomfort are entirely tolerable, at the end of the day. They often only become a problem when you treat them like a catastrophe.

One way to learn that discomfort won't kill you and you'll be fine is to purposefully lean into discomfort. Find ways of safely adding discomfort to your life.

Today, make a list of activities that you avoid because they are uncomfortable. These can include activities of many sorts. Some people are uncomfortable when they're cold, like walking in the snow, and some people aren't comfortable speaking in public. Everybody has something that makes them uncomfortable. Some of the things that make us uncomfortable are actually dangerous, but far more of them are just a little bit unpleasant.

When you have a list of things that you would otherwise avoid, make a commitment to pushing yourself to confront these uncomfortable things. Try to fit something uncomfortable in each day. Some days, go out of your way to do something deeply uncomfortable. It can be as small as taking a cold shower or as big as speaking to a stranger. By forcing yourself to do uncomfortable things you make yourself more comfortable with discomfort. This exposure will diminish the negative feelings that are experienced when you aren't comfortable.

When you do something uncomfortable, make a point to rationally analyze the experience. Everyday moments of discomfort are not catastrophes. When you experience discomfort, you learn that you can survive anything you experience. The discomfort that you undergo actually makes you stronger. You learned something whenever you have an unpleasant experience.

Learn to express the gratitude to the discomfort. When you walk outside without a jacket, thank the cold for testing you and helping you grow. That cold is making you stronger. Most people can't bear to be uncomfortable, but this experience of discomfort is helping you grow beyond them.

Push yourself in all sorts of little ways. When it is cold, we're a code that is too thin. Eat food that you find unpleasant or that you do not like. If kale is not something he would normally choose, have a big plate of it for dinner. Start your morning with a cold shower. Wake up early and let yourself be tired.

Please, tiny discomforts should be embraced with as much joy as you can manage to have. They may be unpleasant but you are thriving. You aren't doing something difficult and pushing yourself as a human being. It is a good thing to push yourself. The ability to push ourselves is what makes us human and excellent. Force yourself to smile when you are cold or hungry. That smile will help you feel more at ease and help you shift your attitude

When you learn to shift your attitude and embrace discomfort, you will grow to be a better person. The ability to be comfortable with discomfort will help you master anything you want to do. Exercise becomes easier. Eating healthy will be more approachable. You will be able to travel with more comfort. Self-discipline depends on the ability to tolerate discomfort.

When people eat junk food instead of healthy food they do so because they find healthy food uncomfortable. Vegetables are less pleasant than candy, so people eat candy. When people avoid exercise because it makes them sore, they are avoiding discomfort. It can get even worse. Some people distract themselves from discomfort by doing things that are bad for them. They might eat or drink too much in order to avoid thinking about the hard time they're having.

Don't do that. Learn to embrace difficulty. When you practice not only accepting discomfort but actively going out of your way to being uncomfortable you will learn to push yourself further. When you experience discomfort, grief that moment with gratitude and joy. In most of modern life, we are very comfortable. We don't often have the chance to be safely uncomfortable. You should be grateful when that occurs.

Day 6:
Meditate

Mindfulness and meditation can have huge benefits to every part of your life. The term mindfulness is commonly used in contemporary Western psychology, but it derives from the ancient tradition of Buddhism. Mindfulness develops enhanced awareness of moment to moment mental processes. When you are more aware of how your mind works, your perception will increase, you will reduce negative emotions, and you will be able to improve your coping skills.

Mindfulness means paying attention and without judgment. Meditation is an important form of mindfulness, but mindfulness can be incorporated into the whole of your life. Research shows that mindfulness will help you in all aspects of physical and mental health. Mindfulness decreases stress, helps your heart, and improves your sleep. When you are mindful, you will work better at your job and be more productive. It has been shown to increase job satisfaction and decrease the sense of emotional exhaustion.

Mindfulness is a crucial aspect of self-discipline. Even if you already have self-control, mindfulness will help you increase your well-being and decrease your sense of distress. Mindful people are better able to control themselves. When scientists look at the brains of people who practice meditation, they see physical changes that correspond to increasing both cognitive abilities and emotional control.

Learning to meditate will help you increase your focus which will help all aspects of your productivity. Meditation is the art of increasing our ability to focus. Focus is a prerequisite of all tasks. Whenever you try to do something difficult, you must constantly return your attention to that thing.

Meditation, at its core, is very simple. All you have to do is sit quietly and focus on your breath. When your mind inevitably gets distracted and leaves your breath, simply return your conception to the breath. Getting lost in thought is not a problem for meditation because improvement happens when you bring your attention back to the breath. The goal is to return your attention to the breath over and over again until the timer sounds. As you practice this, your ability to focus and concentrate will improve.

Make sure that you do not get frustrated or upset with yourself. Your mind will wander—that is what minds do. Your job is to simply return it to the task, kindly and gently. When it wanders, that is your chance to learn to increase your focus. Focus entirely on the breath. You can focus on any aspect of it. Try keeping your attention on how the air feels as it enters and exits your nose or the movement of your chest as it inflates and deflates. For some, it is easier to count the breaths and focus on the numbers. Try counting up on each inhale and exhale, until you reach ten, and then start it over again. At first, do not adjust your breathing in any way—just breathe naturally and observe the pace.

In order to meditate, all you need is something to sit on and a timer. You can sit on anything. For some, it is easier to sit on a chair, upright. Others prefer to sit on a cushion cross like it, which is more traditional. Regardless of the position that you hold, sit with alertness and comfort. Sit up straight and make sure that your back maintains some amount of tension. You don't want to fall asleep when you are meditating.

Your eyes can be open or closed. For most, keeping your eyes closed makes it easier to concentrate. But if you find yourself falling asleep, keep them open and maintain your focus on the middle distance. Let your eyes rest gently on something in front of you. Do not worry about your hands. They can rest on your legs if that is comfortable for you.

For a timer, use your phone. Make sure you turn off any notifications. Notifications will interrupt you and distract you from the meditation that you are trying to engage. Set the timer and have a calming tone for the alarm. If you have something too abrupt, then it will be unpleasant and shocking to interrupt your meditation. There are many apps available for guided meditation if that is something you prefer. You can find guided meditations on YouTube, where someone will walk you through the meditation and help you focus. However, even if in general you prefer guided meditation, it is very useful to be able to meditate silently on your own.

Research shows that meditating longer has increased beneficial effects. The important thing is to meditate every day because it is in establishing a habit that the benefits will occur. Try to meditate each and every day for twenty minutes. For most people, it is important to establish a specific time which will be the meditation time in your day. Try meditating immediately after you wake up before you even make a cup of coffee. Alternately, you can meditate before bed, in order to relax for sleep. If you meditate in the middle of the day, think of it as a break to help you relax and refocus on your work.

In addition to trying out meditation, incorporate mindfulness into your daily routine. Most of us go into autopilot as we do the day-to-day tasks of living, such as brushing your teeth or cleaning the dishes. Try focusing exactly on what you are doing. Do not let your mind wander to anything else. Feel the sensations of the toothbrush. Taste exactly what the toothpaste tastes like. Focus in on what is happening to you and be fully present in the moment.

One good strategy is to learn to eat mindfully. Many of us eat while on the computer or our phone. We eat in front of the television or mindlessly while we are watching a movie. Try to avoid doing this. When you are eating, focus only on eating. This will make your food more pleasurable and fulfilling. You will be able to fully experience the things that you are tasting and learn to enjoy them fully. Look closely at the food. Analyze exactly how it smells. When you chew, do so thoroughly and really consider the taste of the food. This can often be a helpful way to eat less and healthier.

Day 7:
Control Emotions

Our lives are full of things that we cannot control. Traffic happens to us. When our partner fights with us, they say things that we may not like. Our boss gives us orders and we have to follow them. There are so many things which are entirely out of our power.

Most people think of their emotions as outside of their control in that way. We think of emotions as something that overcomes us. Something happens in the world and it causes us to feel a certain way. When someone cuts us off in traffic, it makes us angry. We discuss it in the language of cause and effect. The cause is an event in the world and the effect is a particular emotion in our minds.

In reality, we have control over our emotions. There is a space between the cause and the effect. Events in the world are outside of our control, but we have the ability to control our interpretation of the event. Things happen and then we make judgments about them. We think about the world and we interpret it. Those thoughts and interpretations are what leads to having particular emotions.

If you were in a foreign country where you didn't understand the norms and someone made a hand gesture at you, you would not know to be angry. You would have no conception of if that hand gesture was rude. In order to respond angrily, you must form the judgment that the gesture was rude and the corresponding judgment that it is appropriate to respond to rude gestures with anger. You could decide that it is meaningless or funny. You could interpret the gesture as something which will make a good story someday and thereby greet it with pleasure.

The only person who has power over your emotions is you. You are the one who is able to decide if you get angry when something happens to you. There is no absolute requirement that you respond in a particular way to events in the world.

The ability to regulate your emotions is a crucial part of mental health. When you are able to regulate your emotions, you will experience fewer negative emotions and have a better awareness of what you are feeling. It will prevent you from reacting inappropriately or in ways that you would otherwise regret. You will be able to perform better in stressful situations and handle unpleasant emotional reactions.

This ability helps self-discipline in a lot of ways. If you imagine someone who is controlled by their emotions, they are not controlled by their better judgment. They are thrust this way and that on the winds of fate, responding without thought to what happens to them.

The goal is not to suppress your emotions. You should not push down what you experience and deny that it happened to you. Instead, you should be trying to reappraise and evaluate your emotions. When you experience an emotion, acknowledge it and begin to explore the judgments which lead to that emotion. Determine if those judgments--and the corresponding emotional reaction--are useful to you. What is the effect of these judgments and do you support it as part of your life?

If something happens to anger you, do not just shove down that anger. Instead, evaluate if that anger is the appropriate response. Will anger help or harm you in a particular circumstance? Maintain a focus on what is useful to you and beneficial to your life. That is the best way to evaluate what to do or what is appropriate. Any other mechanism--like, is the anger justified? --only begs the question. What makes anger justified? Anger is only justified by particular judgments about a situation. If you think, I am right to be angry because this person cut me off, you are already presuming that it is appropriate to respond to being wronged with anger. What if, however, you focused on what was best for your life? Why waste energy on someone who hurt you, especially if that might just have the potential to make everything worse?

If someone insults you, you are the one with the power to be insulted or not. You can decide to ignore it or you can decide to blow up and create problems for yourself. Once you get in the habit of evaluating and appraising your emotions, you will be able to decrease negative emotional experiences and increase positive emotions. You will be able to think about complicated situations more easily and with a better eye to what will improve your life on the whole.

In order to practice regulating your emotions, today, make time to monitor them. Every half hour, write down what you are feeling in your journal. What emotions are running through your mind? If there is a strongly negative or positive emotion, take the time to analyze why you are feeling that. What is the event that prompted this emotion? What are your judgments about that event that are leading to that emotion?

This act of evaluation will help you develop the ability to respond to your emotions with ease. When you experience a strong emotion, you need to develop the habit of pausing and thinking about it before acting. Many of us leap into action unthinkingly and often create problems for ourselves. In contrast, self-discipline demands that we have the ability to think about what we are going to do and why we are going to do it. We have to have the ability to control our emotions.

Try visualizing difficult experiences in order to practice this skill. If there are certain types of experiences which tend to make you angry or sad, imagine them. Really pretend that you are experiencing the event. Then, evaluate your emotions and practice determining if they are effective and beneficial to you. This skill will be crucial in all aspects of your life, from your work to your love.

Day 8:
Keep Your Life Clean

Research has shown that doctors with the cleanest offices produce the most research. When you are clean, you are more productive. The productivity of individuals who are tidy was part of the same impulse that kept them tidy. People who are clean create order out of chaos and resist the slide into entropy. Dirty people allow themselves to be subject to the slide into chaos. They are unable to maintain their lived environment in a way that presents them in the best light and helps them do what they want to do.

Self-discipline is essential to maintain cleanliness. Whenever you act or do something in a particular location, it naturally becomes messier. When you move objects, you make things unclean. When you produce things, you produce waste. All actions tend toward messiness and disorder. When you try to be clean, you are trying to be in a battle with the natural tendency of the world. This is self-discipline, properly understood. When you try to be self-disciplined, you are pushing yourself to do the difficult thing and do that difficult thing well. Keeping your space clean and neat is a difficult thing, but it is necessary.

Cleanliness involves constant vigilance. Whenever you pick something up, you need to put it back. Always put things back. It is never okay to leave something sitting out with the thought that you will get to it later. Whenever you start allowing yourself to do that, you will end up in a situation which builds on itself and constantly spiraled out of control. Messiness always wants to increase. You must work to combat it.

Research shows that any disorder leads to more disorder. Have you ever heard of "broken windows theory?" This is a theory of policing that says when there are small crimes creating damage in a neighborhood, it makes it more likely that large crimes occur. A broken down neighborhood with dirty lots and broken windows is a neighborhood with more crime. In the same way, leaving a coffee cup out to get dirty and make your space cluttered means that you are less likely to do the hard work of cleaning. When people are in situations where things are already out of place, they are more willing to be messy themselves. Every time you leave paperwork out, you make it more likely that the next bit of paperwork will also be left out.

When you really want to be tidy, you have to maintain constant effort. A once a week clean is not good enough. Every moment takes small opportunities to maintain your space. When you finish a cup of tea, take it to the sink and clean it up. Do that immediately. Do not wait. We often tell ourselves that we did too difficult to maintain our space and that we are too busy to deal with something right away. You must internalize the idea that cleanliness creates time and will make you less busy. When you are clean, you create a space that allows you to work without stress. A cluttered location creates mental clutter that makes everything more difficult. It is impossible to be too busy to maintain cleanliness because cleanliness helps you be less busy.

Having physical order to space means that you will make better choices. Research shows that cleaner people are more likely to choose healthier food, donate more generously, and maintain social conventions like banners more easily. When you have physical order in your space you are more likely to follow instructions and maintain guidelines. Physical order and cleanliness lead to healthier choices and is in general, crucial to all forms of self-discipline. If you want to change your life, you cannot afford to allow your space to become messy.

Even the messiest people among us tried to stay clean for company. It is a familiar sight to see someone frantically picking up close off the floor and cleaning dishes because someone is going to come to their house. Mass, for some people, is only cleaned up when they expect others to arrive in their space. We think it's polite to welcome people to a clean and welcoming space. But there is an important question here. Why do your guests deserve cleanliness? Are your guests more important than you? Anybody in your space is only there for short amounts of time. You, however, lived there. You spend enormous amounts of time in your space. If it is important for guests to have a clean environment, think about how much more important it is for you to have that cleaned up the environment. You are in your home every day. You deserve to have your house looking nice and clean.

Even if you tell yourself you don't care about the mess, you still clean-up for other people. That proves in some sense you do care about the mess. If it truly didn't matter to you, you wouldn't bother to clean up for others. You care about the mess. You just don't care enough to keep it clean for yourself. Think of it this way. You are the most important person in your life. You are the most important person to walk through the doors of your home. If you would clean up with the president or your boss visited you, you should clean-up for yourself. Respect your ability to live in your own space.

So, if you want to decide to be clean, how do you go about doing that?

The most important part of being clean is to have fewer things. The less stuff you have, the easier it is to clean it up. Your first task today is to pick a part of your house, and de-clutter. If you are regularly using something, get rid of it. Have the discipline to get rid of things that you do not need. Go to your closet and take out any piece of clothing that you haven't worn in three months. If you need it for a particular type of weather, you can spare it, but otherwise, be brutal. Prune your life of things that simply take up space. Make sure to spend the time to get rid of something if you do not need it. Today, you are going to sort through some part of your life. Make a pile of things to throw away. Make another pile of things to donate. Last, make a pile of things to keep. Try to keep the pile of things to keep the smallest pile. You want to try to get rid of things. Make it a goal to get rid of as much as possible. Once you have the collection of things to give away or to throw away, ensure that you get it out of your house as soon as possible. It is easy to have a trash bag of things to donate sitting around for months.

Once you are happy with this amount of things that you have, keep methodical track of them and make sure to clean them regularly. Every day clean for at least 20 minutes. Do it in cycles. Clean for 20 minutes and then take a 10-minute break. After you've done that repeat and clean for another 20 minutes. Whenever you try to clean for hours without end, you create something into a marathon which should be a short sprint. It is not sustainable to try to clean that frantically without time for pause. Devote yourself to cleaning piece by piece until your house is in a state where you would be proud to show to visitors.

Day 9:
Embrace Failure

Failure is really scary. We often try to avoid new things because we are afraid to fail them. Many of your worst memories are probably memories of failure. No one likes to be turned down or to make a bad grade on a test. However, the people who succeed the most are also those who fail the most. Thomas Edison built countless light bulbs that did not work before he managed to build one that didn't work. If he was afraid of failure, he never would've built the light ball. JK Rowling, the author of the famous Harry Potter series, was turned down over 12 times. She had to keep going in order to be the person that she wanted to be.

The most challenging moments in your life are actually the greatest opportunities to learn and grow as a person. Hard times, with failure and pain, hold the greatest potential to transform your life for the better. Your dreams and ambitions depend on the ability to fail and fail well. All of us will have a variety of positive and negative experiences. The thing that differentiates successful people from people who wish they were successful is that the successful learn to take advantage of their failures. Moments of struggling can either help us get to new heights or beat us down, depending on how we interpret them and respond.

Life should be understood as constant growth. We should convert moments of failure into times to reflect on our lives and look for lessons in every moment of pain. Negative emotions such as pain, sadness, or anger can contaminate the way that we feel about events in our lives. Something happens to us and we can become overwhelmed by negative emotions. They are natural and human. Negative emotions are unavoidable and necessary. But, you don't have to linger on your sadness and negative emotions. We should be grateful for dreadful moments because they are able to provide us with a new understanding.

Every life is a journey and every single day we have the opportunity to improve. Our goals are always a part of the process of self-development. We each have the power to get better and to become better people. If we are discouraged by failure and alter our course, we will never reach our potential. When you experience failure, take it as an opportunity to evaluate your life and push yourself into new heights. Failure is the greatest teacher. When you fail, you've learned something about your life and what it takes to succeed. When you try something and fail, you learn that you should do the thing in a different way. You might not immediately know what way is the best way, but you know at least one way that doesn't work. If you study for a test and failed that test, you know that you need to study differently. Each failure is one more step closer to your goal.

Failure also means that you've stepped out of your comfort zone. People do not fail at things that they are experienced at, at least not usually. If you've done something countless times, you will likely succeed at it. The times that you fail are the times that you push yourself to do new things. In order to be successful, you have to operate outside your comfort zone. We all have enormous potential, but most people fail to actualize it. Most of us stay within our zones of comfort and expect things to change. However, extraordinary things only happen when you are uncomfortable. Success occurs because you've pushed yourself and found your highest limits. In order to bring out the best in yourself, you must have a no fear attitude toward failure. Learn to try out new things without fearing the outcome.

When you play it safe out of fear of failure, you do an enormous disservice to yourself. You make success impossible when you shy away from the possibility of failure. We often spend enormous quantities of our life considering the possible outcomes that will harm us and we convince ourselves that any risk would be disastrous. But, we are all braver than we expect to be. Today, make it your goal to do the more daunting things first. Do the scary thing. Lean into fear. Instead of trying to fight against possibilities of failure, push yourself to possibly fail.

Today, do something you know you will fail at. Go to a group that is conducted in a language that you barely speak. Take an exercise class that is well above what you normally do. In general, look for a situation that you don't think you will be able to succeed and do it. It is hard to put yourself in situations like this. Most of us work most of the time in order to avoid failure. However, pushing yourself in that way will help teach you just how much is possible. I am positive that you will do better than you expect to do, even if you still fail. That failure is good. Lean into fear.

At the very least, failure will help keep you grounded. Failure inevitably hurts your ego. We all like to think that we are capable people, who can do what things we want to do. But failure, as painful as it can be, reminds us that we are only human. When you succeed, your ego is fed, and you often blind yourself to your flaws or mistakes. It is hard to see things honestly when all you see is success. When you fail, you are more likely to reach out to others and learn from them. It encourages you to seek expertise outside yourself. It also reminds you that you are only human. This will be able to be a way you can interact with others. You will learn to be sympathetic to not only your own failure but the failure of others. When you accept mistakes and learn from them, you will learn to taste success the next time around.

The way you handle failure determines what sort of person you are. Many people take failure personally and give up. When you give up quickly you encouraged your own stagnation in life. When you learn from failure, instead of letting it get you down, you will be able to go far. Failures should be understood as a temporary obstacle and not something which dooms you. Even though you might feel bad when you fail, it is a great opportunity to develop strength of character. The way you respond to failure determines what sort of person you are.

Day 10:
Embrace Rejection

Most people are terrified of rejection. It is really difficult to be vulnerable and to be told no. In general, a lot of people go out of their way to avoid rejection. They do not ask for things. They do not ask for people on dates. Instead of putting themselves out there and asking for what they want, they instead fold in on themselves and avoid the possibility of rejection.

Being liked and accepted is pleasant. We want to have friends and we want our friends to like us. We often worry that if we act incorrectly, we will lose everything. Any rejection becomes proof that everything could come crashing down on us at any moment. We view rejection as a sign that we are worthless or inadequate. A lot of our self-worth is placed in how people respond to us and it becomes unacceptable that people reject us. For some people, this painful fear of rejection can manifest in anger. For some people, when they are turned down, they lash out and attack the person that has told them "no". This is not a healthy way to respond to the word "no".

When you are rejected, the appropriate response is to look at yourself and discover why. It is important to take seriously the value of the other person and whoever turned you down. When you are rejected, do not take this as a reason to think that you're a bad person. All it means is that what you've asked for is not what the other person wants to give. It's important to get past the fear of rejection. When you are self-disciplined, you will put yourself into positions where rejection is possible. That is the nature of self-discipline.

Living bravely means that you will be rejected. If you submit your work, sometimes you will be turned down. If you ask someone attractive on a date, sometimes they will say no. Every time you are brave and putting yourself out there, there is the possibility that you will be rejected. Rejection is the price of asking for what you want. Applying to a job that you desire and that will make you happy always contains the possibility of rejection. It's we all know that we might be rejected when we put ourselves out there. But just knowing that we will get rejected and actually getting rejected are different things entirely. Even if you know rejection is a possibility, the actual experience of rejection can be enormously painful. We tell ourselves we can handle criticism, but the actual criticism makes us feel small. Rejection cannot us to the ground and leave us unable to catch our breath. We can feel dizzy from shame and inadequacy. Rejection can make us think "what is the point?"

Research shows that rejection triggers the same parts of our brain as physical pain does. Rejection hurts. It hurts in a similar way that pain hurts. The brain activates and responds such that you feel negative things. It is easy to feel like we do not belong when we are rejected. Rejection cuts deep because it makes us question whether or not it is appropriate for us to be doing the thing that we are doing. If you tell someone that you love them and they replied that they don't feel the same way, it is easy to feel like you don't actually belong in that relationship.

There is an enormous risk that we let this emotional fallout of rejection prevent us from trying again. It hurts to be turned down. Sometimes, people respond to this hurt by avoiding the possibility of rejection. However, the only way to get what you want is to ask for it. And the only way to get what you want is to be willing to be told no. You only get yes when there is a possibility of no. You demonstrate courage and bravery by asking for what you want and submitting yourself to the possibility of rejection.

When you get rejected, take a day off. Let yourself be sad. But dust yourself off and get back to it. Do not let yourself give up for longer than just a little to recover. You work hard and you put yourself into situations. This means that you owe it to yourself to put yourself in positions where you can get rejected. Rejection won't kill you. Even being told no hundred times won't kill you. It will suck. You will not enjoy being rejected. But, it is only through rejection that you can get what you want.

Rejection is something that you can practice. Specifically, put yourself into situations where you will get rejected. Submit something that you know isn't good enough and will get you told no. Ask someone out who you think is above your league. Get practice in the process of being told no. The more nos you get, the easier it will be able to hear one without flinching.

Today, take some time to journal about rejections in your path. We all have experiences of rejection. Think of three moments where you've been rejected. Take the time to describe to yourself exactly what happened and how you felt about it. Once you consider the event, remind yourself what you did instead. What opportunities were opened up in your life because you were rejected? How did you grow because of that rejection? Did you get an acceptance later? Many times, we will discover that rejection isn't the end of the world and actually makes it more possible to succeed in the future. Whenever a door closes another one opens.

There is always a possibility. Learn to find those possibilities.

In addition to the journaling, put yourself out there today. Ask for something that you want. Maybe it is from your work. Maybe there's a privilege or benefit that you've been wanting and today's the day to ask for it. There is that pretty quarter office or that nice raise. Be polite and reasonable but you will never get what you want unless you ask for it. Learning to ask for you want is an enormously important skill in the process of success.

Day 11:
Prioritize and Delegate

In general, self-discipline is about doing what you intend to do. It is about making golden actualizing them. However, before you make a commitment, it is important to decide if that commitment is something you actually want to do. You must control the commitments that you make and what you promise to people. Every time you make a commitment, you make a choice to do something. You should commit to things that you really want and that are in line with your values. It is important to have a strong sense of what you need in order to determine what you should do.

Even among the commitments that you have, you don't always need to do everything. The ability to prioritize and delegate is an important part of self-discipline. When you lead a team especially, your primary job is to manage the other members of your team and distribute tasks in line with their talents. When you feel like you have to do everything yourself, you actually are acting in a counterproductive way. A part of self-discipline is knowing when did life go and when to say no. You need to be able to determine what is the most important task among a variety of tasks and who should do that task.

Prioritization depends on the idea of finding the most important thing in doing that thing first. You must organize your tasks such that the most important ones get the highest amount of attention. It is often difficult to do this because everything feels like it is important. It becomes difficult to choose how to start. When you are leading a team, there are often many different opinions about what the most important thing is. This makes it especially difficult to prioritize.

As a team, do the after prioritization with the group. You need the ability for everyone to body and then commit to the prioritization. Get together as a group and list all the necessary tasks in a larger project. Make sure to list even small tasks, because it is important to know what you actually need to do to get the things done. Once you have the larger list of tasks, identify a subset of them that count as "high priority" and put those cast in a separate list. Do not just isolate the absolute most important tasks. There is always a subset of tasks which are necessary in order for the larger project to succeed. Those high priority tasks should be delineated and made explicit.

With this list of high priority tasks, budget your time. Take the time to determine how long each task will take. How many man-hours will be necessary to do the things that need to be done? This is a good place to start to think about delegation. Different people are able to do different tasks with more ease. An individual who is particularly skilled in a certain task will be able to complete it faster than another individual. The people that do things faster should do those things. Delegate with the mindset that you want people to be doing what they do best. Even if someone is a generally diligent and hard worker, you must prioritize tasks such that people are working less hard more efficiently. It is better for someone to do something that they find easy than for them to work hard and show that they are committed to the team.

This means learning to be familiar with the specific skill sets of your team. You should be familiar with the strengths and weaknesses of everyone you are in charge of. Even though most of this chapter is talking about what to do at work or if you are a leader in your job, this will be true in any group of people. Even in the family, there are people who have different skills and competencies. Maybe you are really good at cooking. In general, people tend to do things like alternate chores. But it is much more efficient to have people do the chores they excel at and find most pleasant. If I really hate cooking, I shouldn't be forced to cook just because of fairness. This is especially the case if I really like laundry and my partner does not.

In this sense, being a good leader and learning to delegate tasks is part of being a good friend. You must learn to understand those people around you and take seriously their wants and needs. Listen to what people are saying they want to do and what they excel at.

Part of delegation is learning to release control over the situation. Even though you may be responsible for the success of the operation, it is often valuable to let other people make decisions. It benefits the entire project if everyone involved can make decisions. If too much power is concentrated in one person, the environment loses balance and the ability to be flexible. Share small decisions especially those that do not have large effects. Become capable of allowing those underneath you to take power over what they are doing. Trust the skills and competencies of those that are underneath you. If you find that you cannot trust them, evaluate whether or not you have the right team and if you should be doing something differently in hiring.

Today, as part of the process of prioritization, create a 4 x 4 quadrant. Urgency should be on the x-axis and importance on the y-axis. Under high importance, high urgency (quadrant one) will be emergencies and things that need to be dealt with immediately. Under high importance, low urgency (quadrant two) will be working that affects the larger course of your environment. This is important in determining the values and goals of the organization. Under low importance, high urgency (quadrant three) will be typical daily tasks that need to get done in order to keep the lights on. The last quadrant is low importance, low urgency (quadrant four) and involves things that will be at the bottom of your list. These are things that may be and sometimes need to get done, but it's not crucially important for them to get done right away.

This project of classifying things in terms of their urgency and importance helps you determine where to spend your time. Even though self-discipline will help you spend your time more efficiently, time is still a limited resource and something that you need to take seriously. Once you learn to prioritize and delegate, your self-discipline will be even more powerful. It will be the case that you will be able to do more with less.

Day 12:
Positive Self-Talk

Our brains constantly tell us things. We all have messages that play over and over in our mind. We have an internal dialogue or personal commentary that frames the way that we react to the world and understand things that happen to us. In order to recognize and sustain optimism, hope, and joy, we must consciously and purposely make our self-talk positive.

This is a crucial process of self-discipline, because it pushes back against the conception that self-discipline is about punishing yourself. Many people think that self-discipline is about being harsh. We have talked about how self-discipline involves sometimes choosing to do the uncomfortable thing. That doesn't mean it is punishment, however. Self-discipline is about making yourself a better person. This means it is a project of happiness and self-development. You should gain joy in self-discipline. Joy should help you learn to be a better and more self-disciplined person.

For most people, the way that we talk to ourselves is very negative. It is easier to remember negative things than it is to remember positive things. Our brains are hardwired to remember things that are dangerous and often we remember criticism and failure as dangerous in the same way the bear might be dangerous. We remember negative reactions from our parents or teachers. These messages play over and over in our minds, often fueling feelings of guilt and hopelessness.

Especially for people with depression, these patterns of negative self-talk become damaging and self-destructive. We learned that we are hopeless in the failures because we constantly tell ourselves that we are hopeless. We need to learn that we are valuable and replace the sense of worthlessness with a felt experience of our own value. You may not suffer from depression, but I am sure that you are often critical of yourself and find yourself to be someone who doesn't succeed in the way that you want to do.

As an experiment, write down some of the negative messages that you tell yourself. If something goes wrong or you are rejected what do you say to yourself? Be as specific as possible. What are the things that run through your mind when difficult things happen? Take some time to include any individual who you think you are echoing with these negative thoughts. Are your thoughts reminiscent of something that your parents or teachers have told?

After you've taken the time to write down these negative messages, counter them with positive truths about your life. For every negative message, there is a positive thing that can counter it. There is always a possibility that can override despair. Keep looking for these truths and you will find them.

For example, you might tell yourself that "you can't do anything right" when you make a mistake. This might derive from things you've heard in childhood. However, you can replace that negative messaging with a positive way of viewing the mistake. Instead of saying that you can't do anything right, tell yourself "I choose to grow for my mistake" or "my mistakes made me a better person." In this view, mistakes become opportunities to enhance yourself.

This positive self-talk isn't lying to yourself. It doesn't mean that you are not viewing the world as it really is. Instead, positive self-talk is about recognizing the truth and positivity in your life. It is about seeing things more accurately and recognizing that every negative experience is, in fact, a positive experience and an opportunity to grow. Expecting perfection from yourself is unrealistic. All people will make mistakes and experience failures. However, it is exactly those failures that make us the person that we are and help us grow into new possibilities.

Everybody likes praise and everybody likes to feel good. When you do something positive, make sure to remind yourself that you did well. Write down that you did something beneficially and really reinforce it. Make sure to take the time to praise yourself and reflect on your accomplishments.

You can choose to be a positive person. Your thoughts are within your control. Make a commitment to be optimistic and to view things in the positive light. Focus on your value as a person and the things that you can contribute to the world. Everyone has things where they wish they could be better. But if you only focus on those things, it will become difficult to see the things that make you beautiful.

You can teach yourself to be a positive person. Today, make the time to focus on positivity. First, construct positive affirmation. Determine a couple of sentences that reflect the way that you want to see yourself as a positive, optimistic person. This could be focused on things like "I am a worthwhile human being" or "I am capable of doing the things that I want to do." Discover what you want to affirm about yourself and write those things down. These affirmations can become tools for you to help yourself develop positive thinking.

You can even make a cheesy sign with one of these affirmations on it and post it somewhere prominent. You might want to roll your eyes, but actually writing something out and decorating it in a pretty way can help you. It will remind yourself that you are a good, productive person and that it is valuable to take yourself seriously. Reinforce to yourself that the person you are is a good one. Spend some time making the sign look nice and like something that you value. It will reflect the value that you want to place in yourself.

Your last task today is to make a list of your good qualities. Take the time to remind yourself what an awesome person you are. List out the things that you like about yourself. Often, this can feel very difficult, but force yourself to take it seriously. If it is difficult for you, imagine speaking in the voice of a friend of yours. What would your friends say about you? What are the positive things that your parents might say about you? If that doesn't help, imagine yourself in the position of your own friends. If your friend is with you, what would you say about that? What are your good qualities from the perspective of an outsider?

This list of positivity in these affirmations that a few constructs will help you change your thoughts and feelings into one just support your process of self-development.

Day 13:
Reshape Beliefs That Limit You

The possibilities in your life are shaped by what you believe. Your mind is enormously powerful. The things that you think influence how you perceive the world and what you are capable of. The underlying beliefs that you hold determine everything about your life. Until you make a change in the way that you think about the world, it will be impossible to change your life.

Think of the way you think about the world as a map. Your belief structure is a map that tells you where to go and how to interpret new information. Your belief structures your life. If the map is the same, you will never be able to escape it. With that in order to get to a new destination, you need a new map. Beliefs are like a self-fulfilling prophecy. Believing something to be true, will make it true. You will act to make the things you believe true.

Most people get the same results year after year. They make the same New Year's resolutions and failed to achieve them. The people who are able to make change are those that are able to change their paradigm. A paradigm is the "operating system" of your brain. Your computer may run Windows or Mac but your brain runs a paradigm. This paradigm shapes your subconscious and determines every decision you make.

Most of the time, we are acting purely out of habit. We do not think about most of the things we do. What you do when you make dinner, what you do when you drive to work, what you do when you wake up in the morning — all of these things are automatic and under the control of the subconscious mind. What you hold as a paradigm shapes what you do when you are consciously thinking about things. Your paradigm is able to change your perception of the world.

In order to increase your self-discipline, you have to change your paradigm. This means letting go of beliefs that limit you. How are paradigms formed? Throughout your life, paradigms are created by repetition. Your paradigm was influenced by your parent's paradigm. This is because you continually heard messages from your parent's paradigm as a young child. Especially when you are very young, repetition can shape what you think. Messages go directly to your subconscious mind. When you are told something as a young child, it becomes a seed planted.

In order to determine your paradigm, you must ask yourself questions about your life. Ask yourself: what is your purpose? Does every day have a strong purpose? Are you able to keep focused? Is your life what you want it to be? If you aren't happy with the answers to these questions, it is necessary to change your paradigm. The only way to have self-discipline is to have a paradigm that is consistent with high self-discipline.

Make a list of limiting beliefs that harm you and prevent you from achieving your goals. Some limiting beliefs can include: it is impossible for me to be happy; bad things that can happen will always happen; life is always hard for me: you only get one shot; I'm helpless; nobody loves me; I don't deserve success; it is impossible; I am incapable; I will not succeed.

These beliefs hurt you. They make it less likely that you succeed. They make you unhappier. Limiting beliefs determine the contours of possibility and change what you can actualize in your life. Replace limiting beliefs with empowering ones. Some examples of empowering beliefs include: I am in control of my own destiny; only I can decide what hurts me; life is beautiful; everything happens for a reason; things will turn out well in the end; I can do it; every problem is a learning opportunity.

How do you change a paradigm? The best way to do so is to follow the same practice through which it was formed: repetition. You have to expose yourself to the new idea and new belief, over and over again, until the old limiting beliefs are replaced. Taking the belief that you want to incorporate into your life and repeat it. Write it down over and over in your journal. Record yourself saying it and listen to it as you drive in the car. Make the new belief become part of your inner monologue until it is impossible for you to disbelieve it.

Changing limiting beliefs is the basis of all other interventions and ways of increasing self-discipline. It is hard to do difficult things until you believe it is possible to do difficult things. One way to help yourself incorporate the positive and empowering beliefs into your life is through the process of visualization. Visualization is about imagining new things in such great detail that you essentially fool the brain into thinking that it is real. The brain is very smart, but it is also in some sense very down. Resurgent athletes demonstrate that when you vividly imagine something you can actually shape the part of your brain in the same way that physical practice does. Thinking really hard can change your brain.

Take one of the new beliefs that you want to incorporate and think in great detail about the sets of choices and results that you would want as a result of that belief. If you truly believe this new thing, what would you do instead? Imagine the new behavior as part of yourself and visualize what you would be like if you truly believe this thing. Who is the person that believes these empowering things? How are they different than you? Really incorporate the lived knowledge of what it would be like to believe the empowering beliefs. Once you understand that, it will be much easier to incorporate the belief into your actual life.

Day 14:
Restructure Your Relationship to Technology

One thing we often forget is that technology is just a tool. Our phones and computers feel much bigger and more important than a screwdriver. The phone feels like it is our friendship and our brain. We feel like technology is our connection to knowledge itself because we can find out so much so quickly.

But the thing is, a phone (or any other piece of technology) is just a tool. Tools are only so good at what they are used to do. A screwdriver can be used to put something together or take it apart. You can use a hammer to smash a window. A hammer is only as valuable is how you use it. We often get trapped in technology as being important for its own sake. But technology can either enhance or destroy your life.

Technology can be used to communicate and enrich the lives of others. On the other hand, technology can lose you in the meaningless babble of social media. You can use your phone to take lovely photographs of the world around you or you could endlessly scroll through status update and selfies and ignore that world.

Part of self-discipline is evaluating your relationship with your tools. The world around you should be constructed so that you are the best person you could be. The things in your life should help you meet your goals. You should be helped by your possessions. If you are not, then that means you need to change something about how you interact with your possessions. It is not the answer to completely avoid technology, but to think about instead how to make technology work for you and make your life valuable.

The purpose of advertising is to try to convince you that you need the fanciest in most upgraded version of the technology. We tend to want things just because they are the newest and best. We purchased a new computer, telling ourselves that it is the computer that makes us productive. We say that if we just had the right tool, we would do so much more. This advertising creates a sense of urgency that pushes us to spend money that we do not need to spend in pursuit of making ourselves better. The reality is, it's never the objects in technology that make us more productive. It is only how we use technology that makes us productive. Try to realize that your current objects and technology are working fine. You do not need to own something new. If your current relationship to technology is failing you, that doesn't mean you need a new object. It means that you need a new routine.

Our phones in particular often create habits which cause us pain and make us less productive. We are often entirely and constantly attached to the world of technology. We are continually checking social media and updating ourselves on news. There is a constant stream of notifications alerting us to what we need to know. Our phones vibrate and give us the pressure of updates, making us continually talk to work and friends and everyone who pains us. Instead of meaningful experiences and productive work, we have been all text messages about nothing and pointless emails we have to respond to immediately.

We are programmed by our phones. We continually reach for that phone so many times an hour, checking to see if there is something we should do. But just as you are programmed, it is possible to reprogram yourself. You are able to remove the habits of your life by evaluating what they do for you.

Tech is currently very pervasive. Because of our technology, we never have downtime. We are continually connected to those around us. This will feel like you are being productive but often means you simply never have time to think and process the things you have to be doing.

Constant multitasking is actually making you less productive. When you are trying to work, you probably have notifications of new emails constantly pop up and vibrations from your phone informing you of various things. It is hard to get good, legitimate work done, in the face of all these distractions. Things like email, often feel productive, but you are getting paid to reply to email. It is a distraction from the real work that is important for you to do.

The reality is, multitasking makes you less productive. Learn to focus on one thing at a time. If you have to do something, turn off notifications. Reserve a specific time in your day to do things like answer email, and refuse to answer and any other time but that. In order to get stuff done, it is necessary to shut out distractions. Keep your mind in the present and learn to focus on what you are doing. Single-tasking is a skill that is necessary in order to be as successful as you want to be.

One thing you can do right now, today, is changing the notification settings on your phone and computer. Remove as many pop-ups and notifications as you can. Alerts are almost never necessary. You can always go to check your email directly. Why you need to know when you receive a new email immediately? You can always directly check your email at a certain point in the day. The same thing is true about text messages, tweets, Snapchat, or anything that intrudes on your life.

Day 15:
Eat Better and Count Your Calories

Learning to eat better is one of the most important things you can do to improve your productivity. Our bodies are run on fuel. Much like any machine, the quality of the fuel determines how efficiently and successfully the machine will run. If you aren't eating the right things, your body and mind will not function properly. If you eat too much, you will gain weight and have all of the health problems associated with obesity. Research shows that one of the most prominent health problems in the United States today is obesity. Obesity not only affects your physical health, but it also damages your mental health and cognitive function. It is crucially important to learn to eat well and to keep your body healthy.

Nutrition is fundamentally about variety. It is important to eat many different types of things, especially fruits and vegetables. Fruit has lots of vitamins and many good things for your body. Eating a whole fruit gives you not only the vitamins but also the fiber-fill you need. Things like juice are essentially just sugar and are not nearly as beneficial as a whole. Even more important than fruit, eat more vegetables. Vegetables are better for you than fruit. Vegetables are lower in calories and sugar. Vegetables are also extremely nutrient-dense. They have all sorts of vitamins and minerals that are an essential part of a healthy diet. In order to diversify the vegetables that you are eating, try to eat different colors of vegetables. The colors are clues about the vitamin and mineral content of the vegetables. Dark green vegetables, for instance, have a great deal of iron. Orange vegetables, like sweet potatoes, are a good source of beta-carotene.

Most people aren't as fond of vegetables as they are of things like sugar or meat. Cheese is always going to be tastier than a piece of broccoli. This is why self-discipline is so important. If you just eat what you want to eat, you will eat healthily. Our brains and bodies were evolutionarily affected by scarcity. For much of human history, things like refined sugar were extraordinarily rare. There just weren't as many calories available to the average person. This means that your brain is trained to search for as many calories as possible. However, right now, there are as many calories as anyone could want available for not that much money at all. This means it is important to push yourself to be in control and focus on healthy foods like vegetables.

In addition to vegetables, eat plenty of whole grain. It is important to eat whole grains instead of refined grains like white bread or sugar, because whole grains have more fiber, nutrients, and affect your blood sugar less quickly. The glycemic index, a measure of how quickly foods affect your blood sugar, is a useful guide to determine what foods you should focus on and eat.

Eat less meat and dairy. For most people, especially in the West, meat and dairy are crucial parts of the diet. However, these foods have a lot of calories and are often very dense in fat. Dairy can be quite useful, especially because it contains calcium and vitamin D. These things are essential to keeping your bones strong. However, it often has a quite significant portion of fat that isn't the enemy. Fat is crucial for the functioning of our brain and bodies. However, when you eat fat, trying to eat it from vegetable sources and focus on unsaturated fat.

Unsaturated fat is better for your heart. Meat, even lean meat, is associated with negative health outcomes such as colon cancer. Red meat especially is heavily associated with cancer. As much as possible, eat nonmeat protein such as beans and nuts. If you want to eat meat, focus on poultry.

In general, the most important piece of advice is to eat less. Most of us to eat too much. We eat until we are stuffed and uncomfortably full. It is a useful strategy to try to always leave food on your plate and take a smaller portion. Stop eating before you are fully satisfied. The thing about modern life is that we will never go hungry. It is always possible to get more food. This means there is no need to eat to satisfaction because if you need more food later it is always possible to acquire it.

In order to eat less, it is useful to know exactly what you are eating. The strategy of counting your calories is a useful way to keep your eating in check. Today, your focus will be on counting your calories. Your goal will be to find out exactly what you eat in order to be able to make any changes that are necessary. Even if you do not need to lose any weight it is important to know exactly how much you consume.

There are many apps available that are intended to help you count calories. "MyFitnessPal" is a good app, but there are others. Download one of them and use it to record all the food that you consume. When you are going to eat something, read the information on the package and enter it on the app. If it is not a packaged food, Google how many calories there are in a portion of it and use that to answer it in your app. Many of the apps contained within them calories of common foods.

When possible, use food scale to measure the portion. It is often very surprising to learn how all of our mental sense of portion is. We will find that we eat several portions of rice, for instance, when we think we've only eaten one. The only way you can know how much you are eating is to weigh it. Data will set you free.

Log everything you eat, even if you are embarrassed about it. If you eat a cookie, log it. It doesn't matter if you wish you hadn't have eaten it. You did eat it. That means you log it. The key to change any behavior is information. Without information, you can't know what you need to do. Logging your food will help you have the power to change your behavior.

Day 16:
Embrace Gratitude

Gratitude may seem like a strange topic for a book on self-discipline. However, when you are thankful for what you have, you will attract more things to be thankful for. Gratitude rejuvenates you and helps boost your self-esteem. Research shows that gratitude is a link to both physical and mental well-being. When we embrace gratitude as a daily practice, we feel more positive things and we feel more alive. This means that we express more compassion and kindness to others. Gratitude is what helps us maintain encouraging the feelings and encouraging mindset. When you have a general sense of gratitude, you will be happier and more productive.

Try to establish a daily habit of gratitude. In the morning, sit quietly and reflect on the blessings in your life. Take the time to write in your journal those things that you are grateful for. These can be big things or small things. You can be grateful for your spouse or your children. You could be grateful for Diet Coke. Everyone has something to be grateful for. You may not think your life is going in the way that you wanted to, but there are things about it that you can be grateful for. This list of things that you are grateful for should be an extremely long list. Try to make it almost a competition with yourself. Every time you think you run out of ideas, challenge yourself to write five more things down. The world is a beautiful place, full of good things. If you force yourself to see those good things, you will find that there is an endless list of things to be grateful for.

In addition to spending time journaling, use gratitude right before you go to sleep. If you tend to get worried and anxious when you're in bed, using gratitude can be very helpful. Take the time to mentally think of something you are grateful for while you are in bed getting ready to sleep. When you are grateful, your sleep quality will improve and it will be easier for you to fall into a restful sleep. Having a grateful attitude helps to relax you and makes you feel better.

Grab the goal of lowering stress. Stress is one of the most damaging things on both your body and your mind. Most of us deal with far too much stress in our daily lives. However, gratitude is capable of de-stressing and making us feel better. When you are grateful, you focus on happiness and things that make you feel joy. This will make you abler to cope with the stressors in your life.

Do not condition your gratitude on a certain outcome. Do not tell yourself "I will be grateful when this happens" because doing that will push gratitude forever into the future. It is important to be grateful now, no matter what. You have blessings already in your life. Those good things are important, even if they are not everything you want.

When you feel gratitude, make a point to share it with others. If someone has shown you kindness, remember to pause and thank them for their effort. People often take others for granted. It is easy to not see the work that others do for us. The time taken to pause and make clear our gratitude cannot only increase our relationship with others, but it can also make us feel happier and more satisfied with the life that we have. When you feel gratitude, express it. Do not try to hesitate or wait for a perfect moment. It is never a bad moment to say thank you. When you express gratitude, be specific. Make sure to specifically isolate the thing that the other person did for you and thank them for it. You should express gratitude in its fullness and specificity.

Gratitude can help you through the toughest times. When you list what you are grateful for, it reminds you what you are lucky about. There is always something to appreciate even when times are rough. Being aware of and thankful for all the small joys of life creates a reserve of happiness that is capable of boosting you through even the most difficult times.

Gratitude has a tendency to build on itself. When you get on the habit of expressing gratitude, you will find more things to be grateful for. Noticing the way that your dog greets you in the evening, the taste of your coffee in the morning, the sun in the sky on your skin, a thoughtful email from a loved one — all of these things will help you recognize even more things to be grateful for. The world has a lot of joy in it and it is sometimes difficult to see it. But once you get in the habit of gratitude, you will express more positive energy and withdrawal more positive things into your life. Faithfulness can spiral upward. When you are grateful, you will be happier. That happiness will make you kinder and more compassionate, which means that others will respond to you with more kindness and compassion. This relationship with others will make you even happier and more kind. Use gratitude to springboard a daily routine of joy and connection with others.

Day 17:
Forgive Those That Have Wronged You

Everyone has been hurt in the past. No one makes it to adulthood without being wrong or without experiencing harm done to them by others. Some of us are often distracted by the thoughts of people who have mistreated us. We often think our lives would be better if only someone had behaved differently or hadn't done something to us. However, it is important to accept that the only person responsible for your life as you. Individuals have to take full and exclusive responsibility for their lives. It is crucial to reject the victim mentality and claim power over your own life.

When you credit others as being the cause of your situation, it becomes impossible for you to change that situation. You cannot control anyone or anything but yourself. The only thing that is necessary for change is you. When you blame others for your harms, then you make it impossible for you to solve the problem. In order to create change, it is crucial to place responsibility in yourself.

Psychologists often call this "locus of control." An internal locus of control means that you attribute things to yourself. If you failed a test, someone with a locus of control that is inside themselves with blame themselves. If that locus of control is external, they might blame the teacher. When you have an internal locus of control, you attribute success to your own efforts and abilities. When you expect to succeed, you will be more motivated and more likely to learn. If you attribute your success to fate or lock or other people, you will be much less likely to make effort when you have an external locus of control, you are much more likely to experience anxiety because you believe you are not in control of your own life. Psychologists have found that those who have a more internal locus of control are better off – they tend to achieve more and they have better-paying jobs. Research shows that those with an internal locus of control are less likely to be overweight, less likely to have poor health, and less likely to have high levels of stress. Those with a greater and more internal locus of control behave healthier and have greater confidence in their ability to influence outcomes of their own actions.

It is not useful to be too down on yourself or to criticize yourself too harshly. However, without taking responsibility, it is impossible to change things. A victim mentality says that things in your life are other people's fault. However, if you are not part of the problem, it is impossible for you to be part of the solution. Much like a protagonist in the novel is the center of the narrative, you must make yourself the center of your own life. Refuse to allow yourself to be subject to forces outside of your control.

When you tell the story of your life, tell that story as if you are in control. Take responsibility for your life. This entails that you must let go of resentment and hatred for people that have harmed you. Holding onto bad feelings means that you are holding onto the idea that someone else is the cause of your suffering. The only person that can hurt you is you. The power and that is that the only person necessary to help you is also you. If there are things in your life that you blame on others, evaluate them and try to find a way in which you could make yourself in control.

Your task today is to identify people that you blame for having wronged you. Make a list. Who do you resent? Who in your life do you hold anger for? Write down those people. Take the time to remember the things that you blame them for and evaluate the things that cause your anger.

For each of those people and each of the examples of harm, take some time to determine how you could control that situation. How did you contribute to the problem? How could you have acted to assuage the harm? It is important to recognize that your actions are always part of the situation and that there is nothing that can happen to you without your consent.

In addition, take some time to forgive those people that you are resenting. Speak the words out loud "I forgive you" and send positive energy toward them. Consciously wish them well and make sure you think of good things happening to them. It often helps to repeat out loud: "I wish you happiness. I wish you peace. I wish you flourishing."

By forgiving those that harmed you, you can replace resentment with goodwill. Once you've done that, it becomes possible to reshape your life with you at the center of it. Resentment doesn't harm anybody but yourself. Wishing bad on other people does not make their life worse. It makes your life worse. It drains you and causes you suffering. Even if you are very angry at someone, holding onto that anger only makes your own life more difficult.

Day 18:
Quit When You Need To

Much of this book has been focusing on finishing what you start and doing what you want to do. It is important to learn to push through difficulties. However, success is also dependent on learning when to quit. It is important to be able to give up on something that is not going anywhere.

Unfortunately, there is no magic answer about the right time to quit something. However, it is important to be able to think seriously about the possibility of quitting. It is easy to make errors both by being too quick to quit something as well as by being too willing to go down on a sailing ship.

In many ways, it is more common to refuse to quit when you should. Human beings are naturally loss averse. We are essentially conservative. In general, humans do not like abandoning things. The economic concept of "sunk cost" helps explain this. The sunk cost fallacy is thinking that because you've already spent a great deal of time and effort into something, it is crucial to continue doing it. If I make an investment of $100 into a business, often when the time comes to decide if I should continue investing, I will think that "because I already have money in this, I should keep giving them money." However, this is irrational. If something is a bad investment, there is no reason to keep throwing good money after bad. The sunk cost of the initial investment should not affect the decision to make future investments. The only rational way to decide whether or not to continue to do something is to ignore the sunk cost and just evaluate the possible futures.

It is especially easy to fall into the sunk cost fallacy and things that are important to us. We are very often inclined to just keep trying, as this continued effort will change the result. It is easy to stop on an extra credit project, but it is hard to abandon an entire college degree. It is easy to stop a side gig, but quitting your job is an entirely different matter.

So, how should you make these decisions?

It is crucial to avoid focusing on the time and energy that you have already invested. Making decisions about what you should do should only incorporate what you think the future will be. Always look forward and never look back.

It is also important to avoid over weighing the positive. Because of the sunk cost fallacy, we are incentivized to look for good things and avoid looking at the bad ones. We want to make sure that the things that we have spent effort to succeed. This means that we easily see the good parts of our endeavors and ignore the bad ones. Our brain is trained to look for any possible good interpretation of the situation.

There is also a psychological bias to overvalue things that we have failed. The ex that dumped you is remembered more fondly than the ex that you left. You remember your ex with fondness precisely because they dumped you. In your imagination often the job that you did not get would have made your life perfect. Resist the urge to view possibilities that have failed as if they would have been perfect. It will be much easier to let go of things once you are more realistic about the possibilities.

The most crucial thing, however, is to see the world with a mindset oriented toward attaining success rather than the one that is oriented toward avoiding failure. Your goal should always be to do well, not to avoid doing badly. While at first glance this may seem just like a difference in wording, research shows that this mindset is important. One study gave participants a puzzle that could not be completed and measure how long it took them to get up and move on to the next puzzle. Participants that were oriented toward avoiding failure wasted much more time on the impossible possible. They also had much more intense emotional distress. People who wanted to attain success, however, gave up more quickly when they realize the puzzle would be difficult and moved onto the next one. This gave them more emotional success and correspondingly, more successfully solve puzzles.

When you are focused on attaining success, you will be more willing to do something new when the house is open and worked out. In many cases, we persist in doing something just because we don't want to say that we have failed. But, when your goal is to succeed, it is easier to abandon something that doesn't seem like it will produce success, even if it doesn't quite produce failure either.

Focusing on success has other benefits. If you imagine a big presentation at work, the focus on success might mean that you'll be thinking about how you'll deliver the best possible presentation. If, however, you focus on avoiding failure, you might only be thinking about the ways in which you might embarrass yourself. The failure becomes much more vivid and relevant to your decision-making. When you are focused on avoiding failure, you may persist in something far past the point of rationality. Consider a failing business. Someone who is terrified of failure might try to keep going far past the point where they should've quit and end up losing everything. If you focus on success, you might more quickly realize that this business will not lead to success and move onto the next thing.

Day 19:
Do Something Totally New

For most adults, it has been a very long time since we have done something totally new. Most of us do the same things from day-to-day. We stick to what has given us success in the past and what we are already good at. We are adults, settled in our lives, and we avoid doing things for the first time. We stick to what we are good at and what works.

Try, instead, doing something totally new. Let yourself go out on a limb and do something for the first time. Do not accept the boundaries of your already existing life. There are contours that determine what you acceptably do and what you don't do. Try to ignore them. Do something new. This will help you experience the world in a totally different way.

Self-discipline is about pushing yourself to be the best person you can be. The goal is to develop your skills and capacities enough that you can meet all of your goals. In order to do this, you will have to extend yourself past your comfort zone. In many parts of this book, this does not mean doing entirely new things. Instead, we have talked about doing familiar things in a new way. However, the experience of being genuinely new at something can really help you develop your capacity to stretch yourself.

It makes sense that most of us do what we are already good at. Being good at something is comfortable and rewarding. I am not suggesting that you abandon your already existing life. However, it is a good idea to push yourself. Do not get too comfortable with how you act. One of the things that make us feel old is the abandonment of novelty. New things are exciting and stretch your capabilities. Who knows, you might even find out that you are good at something you did not expect.

It can be difficult to try something new. It is easier to be good at something. But, if you try something new, you will almost certainly not be skilled. Part of the point of doing something new is to experience what it is like to be a beginner. When we were younger, we were beginners in many things. At one point, we had to learn how to do everything we currently do easily. That experience of being inexperienced can be very valuable. It teaches us to be open to possibility and comfortable with the potential to fail. When you do things for the first time, it helps you see the world in a fresh way. Children have a unique perspective on the world. We cannot totally replicate that perspective. But, trying to do things that stretch your potential and your boundaries, can help you view the world in fresh eyes.

When you do something new for the first time, you turn what might be predictable into something exciting. Doing new things can be a lot of fun. It can also be scary. New things are almost by definition outside of your comfort zone. But, pushing yourself past what you find comfortable helps revitalize your life. You will be able to test what your actual boundaries are.

Today, try something totally new. You could do any number of things. You could take a language class in the language you have never spoken before. You could sign up for judo or martial arts. You could smoke a cigar. You could even take a ride on a mechanical bull. Try singing karaoke. Alternately, you can introduce yourself to a stranger. Whatever you do, take fresh eyes into the activity and learn to experience it as a child would. Accept the reality that it will be a little intimidating. You will not be good at whatever it is the first time you try. That experience of being unskilled and without experience can be enormously beneficial and will help you do all sorts of things.

It can be especially valuable to take friends or family along the ride. Try this new thing along with a friend or loved one. That way it won't be quite as intimidating because you won't be doing it alone. This can be especially educating if you take along a child. Children are more used to the experience of being new at something. They can help you be comfortable with pushing your boundaries. Part of the process is learning to see the world out of a child's eyes. Experiencing something alongside a familiar child can help you develop that skill.

In addition to trying something new today, make a list in your journal of additional firsts. Come up with a list of things, big and small, that you have never done before. Make it a goal to add them into your daily life. Continually push yourself to do new things and experience new firsts. Seeing the world in a novel way will help develop your ability to be successful and productive.

Day 20:
Develop A Mentor

All of us can benefit from having mentors. You could be highly advanced in your career or just getting started. In any case, there will be people around who know more than you and who can teach you many things. At the very least, there will be people who have connections that you do not. Mentors can be enormously valuable for learning how to excel in the things that you want to do. In your career, they can be crucial in learning the skills that you need to be productive in the specific context that you exist in.

Even outside of your career, mentors can be helpful. If you are a student, older students have gone through what you currently are experiencing and can have guidance for you. Teachers have seen many students in exactly your position and understand what it is like to be in education. In your personal life, many people who are just starting out in a marriage find themselves reaching out to friends and family that have been married for a long time in order to ask for advice.

Most things that we do in life involve skills and connections that will be able to make them easier. You can always develop yourself and learn more about what your goals are. Like all relationships, however, the relationship with a mentor takes hard work and development. It is important to be able to put the effort in and really nurture the relationship.

Today, try and make a plan to create a new mentor in your life. You will not be able to develop a mentor entirely in one day--this is something that takes time and work. You can, however, think about what you need to do and develop a plan to help you get started. The most important thing is to make a commitment to the idea of finding a mentor and really accept that it is something that will help your life.

As you engage in the process of finding a mentor, try using these tips.

First, identify your goals. A successful mentoring relationship obviously depends on having a mentor! You might have a particular person in mind, but you might not. If you do not know anyone that would be a suitable mentor for you, it is important to be able to think seriously about what type of person will be able to help you succeed. Who could help you develop in the ways that you want to develop? And, more importantly, where might you be able to find that person?

Second, once you have identified a person that could help mentor you, get to know that person. Research them. Learn as much as you can about their personal and professional life. How has their career gone to take them to the point they are currently at? If they are prominent in the public eye, have they given interviews or presented accounts of themselves to the public? It is important, also, to have personal conversations with them. Start to become part of their professional circle. It is impossible to go from being a perfect stranger to having a close relationship without the first stage of being friendly, professional acquaintances.

Third, whenever you interact with your mentor, make sure to follow up. It is crucial to stay in regular contact with your mentor. If you run into them at a conference, send them an email about the encounter. If you have not seen them in a while, send an email. In most situations, it is a good idea to send emails. Try and schedule regular check-ins and conversations. Ask them to have coffee with you or ask if you can buy them lunch. It is important to prioritize face-to-face meetings, which are always the best way to get to know somebody.

Fourth, always present the best possible version of yourself. When you interact with your mentor, make sure that you are fully prepared and enthusiastic. Take the opportunity to show off what a competent and skillful person you can be. The goal is to show them that you are a person they can be proud to have helped. You want to demonstrate that you can be a credit to them and to your field at large.

Fifth, and perhaps most importantly, always take the time to thank your mentor. Gratitude is a crucial part of most relationships and it is especially important in professional mentoring ones. In most cases, you will be getting a lot more material benefits out of the relationship than your mentor. This makes it especially important for you to indicate that you are grateful and that you value their time. Whenever they help you, make sure to thank them. Handwritten notes or small gifts can be particularly impactful in communicating thanks, but even a simple email can be invaluable.

Day 21:
Celebrate Success

Congratulations! Today is the last day of your three-week journey and the first day of the rest of your life. You have worked hard and done many things. You have learned to set good goals and solve problems. You have constructed ways to reward yourself and you have pushed yourself to tolerate discomfort. This whole journey has been oriented around making yourself the best possible person you can be and now, you have completed it. Sometimes focused, driven people like you can be so caught up in what they have left to do that they do not take any time to consider what they have already done.

I am sure there are many things you have succeeded at and not just over the course of this book. Self-discipline and self-development rely on the ability to remind yourself of your successes. This helps you boost your self-esteem and reminds yourself that you are capable of great things. The commitment that success is possible is one of the things that makes self-discipline easier. When you know it is possible for you to do difficult things, it will be easier to focus on the long term at the expense of short-term pleasure. This is at the core of self-discipline.

When was the last time you made space to acknowledge and celebrate your many accomplishments? Often, when we meet a significant goal, we immediately move on to the next one instead of celebrating our wins. This means you will have a higher probability of burning out.

Celebrating releases endorphins inside your body and it makes you feel incredible. It is a reward for all your hard work and it reinforces that hard work pays off with a good feeling. It feels great physically and helps you keep working in the way you have previously been working.

When you fail to celebrate your accomplishments, you actually are training your brain that these things aren't all that important. If everything feels mundane, you will stop having the ability to work as hard and push yourself in the ways you want to push yourself. This will lead to lackluster results and a feeling of emptiness. There will necessarily be less focus and decreased performance as a result.

When you celebrate with others you also increase and develop those relationships. You can throw a party, bringing people who are close to you together and reinforcing those relationships. Even if you do not do anything quite that formal, even mentioning your wins to a loved one or colleague helps to develop that relationship. A celebration can be contagious and it makes other people feel good about themselves and their relationship with you. In addition, reaching out to colleagues creates an opportunity for further collaboration and new ideas. Any excuse to reach out becomes a potential source of new opportunity.

Further, when you celebrate success, you position yourself as a winner. Success attracts more success. People like doing business with people who are winners. When you celebrate, you demonstrate to everyone around you that you are someone who is worth celebrating.

The way you think about the world becomes reality. When you focus on winning, others will look for ways that they can be part of your success. In order to attract valuable people to you, you have to show yourself to be valuable and successful.

It is important not only to celebrate your own successes but also to keep a close eye out for the successes of others. When you recognize the success of employees or loved ones, you encourage and reinforce the determination that got them to that point. You are able to boost their self-esteem and grow the relationship between the two of you. It is very motivating for someone to recognize your success and it will only push your employee to work harder.

Make sure you are prompt and thorough when celebrating the successes of others. It is important to demonstrate that you do not take anyone's hard work for granted. Creating an environment where everyone feels free and empowered to point out the good things that others are doing can only help the productivity of your workplace. You should be the first to notice when an employee does something great. At some point in the future you might want to add a bonus or a gift to the celebration, but even just giving someone a handshake can be enormously valuable for morale.

In addition, it is important to make celebrations public. Recognize in front of others what your employees have done. Send a compliment through reply-all, so that the person you are talking to knows that everyone can see your good regard.

In general, always make time to point out the good things that you or others have done.

Conclusion

Thank you for making it through to the end of *How to Build Self-Discipline: A 21-Day Blueprint to Develop Successful Habits, Increase Your Productivity, Build Daily Self-Discipline and Achieve Your Goals Faster*, let's hope it was informative and able to provide you with all of the tools you need to achieve your goals whatever they may be.

The next step is to incorporate what you have learned into each and every day of your life moving forward. The structure of this book was to use each new day as a learning opportunity to develop your skills and move forward toward your goals. The only way that this changes your life is if you carry that mindset forward with you into the future.

Make sure you keep up with the habits you established during this three-week journey. Continue eating right, getting enough sleep, and finding time for exercise each and every day. Continue using your journal and creating space for self-reflection. In order to develop yourself, you must first know yourself.

This book is just the beginning of the rest of your life. With it, you will be able to climb mountains and conquer your dreams.

Finally, if you found this book useful in any way, a review on Amazon is always appreciated!

Other Books by Judith Yandell

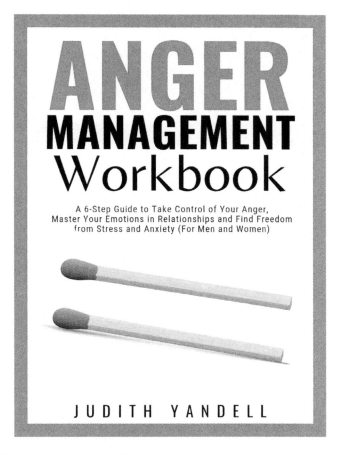

Do you want to take control of your anger and find freedom from stress and anxiety? Here's a 6-step guide that will help you.

Anger will destroy your life. When you're angry you make bad decisions that can ruin your day, damage your relationships or even destroy your career. Here's the sad truth about this: anger is completely natural and you can't just remove it from your life, however…

You can learn how to control and manage your anger in the right way so that you can avoid any form of adverse consequences. See, psychology says that all our reactions are either voluntary or involuntary. In other words... you have a choice. You can either let anger take control of you and damage your life, or you can learn the techniques and strategies to take control of your anger and completely avoid all its bad effects on your body and your life.

If you want to take control of your anger, learn how to manage your emotions and find freedom from stress and anxiety, this 6-step guide is for you.

This isn't a typical book full of nonsense and vague suggestions. "Anger Management Workbook" is an actionable guide that will actually help you manage your anger and improve your life.

Inside Anger Management Workbook, discover:

- A 6-step guide to take control of your anger, master your emotions in relationships and find freedom from stress and anxiety
- Why you can't completely remove anger from your life and what you should be doing instead
- How to detect, handle and take control of your anger in a positive way
- The #1 technique to manage your anger (many people don't know this)

- Why a specific kind of anger can actually help you in many situations (and how to cultivate it)
- The "Iceberg Technique" to effectively understand and control your own anger and that of other people
- 3 highly effective relaxation techniques to manage your anger and avoid negative consequences
- Proven strategies to regain immediate control of yourself whenever you feel angry
- 4 steps to manage your anger successfully, even if you've never tried before
- A complete guide designed to help you recognize, understand and fully control your anger

Learn how to manage your anger and improve your life!

"Anger Management Workbook" by Judith Yandell is available at Amazon.